HEAD ON

Clare Shaw was born in Burnley in 1972. She has published three collections with Bloodaxe, *Straight Ahead* (2006), which was shortlisted for the Glen Dimplex New Writers' Award for Poetry and attracted a Forward Prize Highly Commended for Best Single Poem; *Head On* (2012), which according to the *Times Literary Supplement* is 'fierce, memorable and visceral'; and her latest collection, *Flood* (2018).

She is a Royal Literary Fellow, and a regular tutor for the Writing Project, the Poetry School, the Wordsworth Trust and the Arvon Foundation. She also works as a mental health trainer and consultant and has taught and published widely in the field, including *Our Encounters with Self-Injury* (eds. Baker, Biley and Shaw, PCCS 2013) and *Otis Doesn't Scratch* (PCCS 2015), a unique storybook resource for children who live with self-injury.

Clare lives in Hebden Bridge with her daughter and their two pet rats; she enjoys rock climbing and wild swimming in cold and beautiful places.

CLARE SHAW

HEAD ON

BLOODAXE BOOKS

Copyright © Clare Shaw 2012

ISBN: 978 1 85224 951 9

First published 2012 by
Bloodaxe Books Ltd,
Eastburn,
South Park,
Hexham,
Northumberland NE46 1BS.

www.bloodaxebooks.com
For further information about Bloodaxe titles
please visit our website and join our mailing list
or write to the above address for a catalogue

Supported by
**ARTS COUNCIL
ENGLAND**

Cover design: Neil Astley & Pamela Robertson-Pearce.

Digital reprint of the 2012 Bloodaxe Books edition.

For my daughter and mother.

'There is a light and it never goes out.'

ACKNOWLEDGEMENTS

Acknowledgements are due to the editors of the following publications where some of these poems first appeared: 'I do not believe in silence', *Asylum*; 'Conversations with X and Y', *Magma*; 'Vow', *The Guardian* and *Twenty Poems to Bless Your Marriage*, ed. Roger Housden (Shambala, 2012); 'It could have been', *The Guardian*; 'You', *Some Girls' Mothers* (Route, 2010); 'No Baby Poem', *Answering Back*, ed. Carol Ann Duffy (Picador, 2008); 'Ewe', *Wenlock Poetry Festival Anthology 2011* (Ellingham Press, 2011); 'In the space of that year', *Jubilee Lines*, ed. Carol Ann Duffy (Faber & Faber, 2012).

Thanks to Char March, David Tait, River Wolton, Clare Pollard, George Szirtes, Lou Crosby, Chiara Conway and Joseph Sebastian Shaw. Love and gratitude to Terri, Carol Ann, Lily, Dona, Helen, Ali and Caroline, and all my friends.

CONTENTS

9   I do not believe in silence
11 It could have been
13 Conversations with X and Y
19 Jude got an HGV licence
21 Going going
23 Cupboard
24 French lesson
25 Ewe
27 Night
28 Tree
30 Street Poetry
37 U
38 Recording crime
40 This isn't
41 The no baby poem
42 You
43 Not baby, nor boy
44 You took a tumble
46 Vow
48 The Lesbian Guide to Conception
51 Ewe in several parts
57 In the space of that year
59 She's waited half her life to write this
60 A withered brown flower takes on new colour
62 Ocixem
64 Irreversible
70 You'd start with the page

I do not believe in silence

Because, tonight –
however I try – I cannot get downstairs
without waking my daughter
I do not believe in silence.

Because of the Worboys enquiry,
because of the one hundred-plus women he raped –
because of the policeman defending the findings
unable to utter the word –
'this (herrrrm) crime, this (ahem)
assault, this category (cough)
of offence' –
I do not believe in silence

because of the stairs and the banister's crack;
the sound of the lock
and my hand on the door – the fifty-tone creak –
the magnificent echo of light-switch and click –
I do not believe in silence.

Because of Neda – and everyone's sister –
and the man who said 'Don't be afraid';
for the sake of my daughter, because of the burka,
because of the patter of rain;
because of two hundred thousand years of human history,
thirty-seven of them my own –
I do not believe in silence

for the sake of my arms, the wrists especially.
With respect to my legs
and my belly and chest
and the comfort long due to my throat

because of nightclubs at one a.m.
and shouts in the street and feet in pursuit
and shops that don't shut;

because of sirens and the dealers downstairs;
because of Levi and Akhmatova;
because of the blue-lipped prisoner;
the itch and the scratch of my pen;

I believe in the word.
I believe in the scrabble of claws
on uncarpeted floors.
I believe in my daughter's complaints.
I believe in the violin, the E-string,
the see-sawing bow; the cello
straining its throat.

I believe in the heart and its beat
and its beep and the dance of the trace
on the screen, I believe in the volume
of colour turned up, and my blood
which was always too loud.

Because of the nights, and the sweats,
and the same rowdy thoughts;
because that one afternoon
when I nailed my own voice to the air
and because there was nobody listening
and through it all
birdsong
and the sound of cars passing –

I do not believe in silence.

It could have been

Ali, son of Abdul. 16 months.
Rocket on house, Sadr City 16.5.2009.

Ali, but for some detail of history,
this day could have been yours.

It could have been you this morning,
stood at the end of your bed,
eyes still shut, arms held up for your mother,
who makes sun and all things possible,
who could, little Ali, be me.

Tony Edward Shiol, 5 years.
Kidnapped, found strangled, Shikan 12.05.2009.

If God had sneezed or been somehow distracted;
if that ray of light had shifted
and you had landed
with the small, metallic thrill of conception
as I walked down Euston Road,

then this could have been your morning.
It could have been me inhaling
your breath straight from sleep,
the smell of hot lake and woodsmoke, could have been
my tired arm under your neck.

Unnamed male baby of Haider Tariq Sain.
Car bomb, Nawab Street, Baghdad 7.04.2009.

It could have been you
shouting 'carry'
at the far top stair of my stairs –

hello stairs
hello breakfast

– your feet in these shoes
which do not contain ants;

Unnamed daughter of Captain Saada Mohammed Ali.
Roadside bomb, Fallujah 20.4.2009.

biting soap
which smells good
but does not taste good; watching
the unsteady wonder of bubbles;
throwing water up into the light

Unnamed son of Haidar, 4 years.
Suicide bomber, Baghdad 4.1.2009

then swimming:
your body held out in my hands;
the pear-shaped
weight of your head
safe away from the pool's sharp side

Sa'adiya Saddam, 8 years, female.
Shot dead by USA forces, Afak 7/8 Feb, 2009

It could have been me on that street
with you in my arms
and my hands red and wet
and my face is a shriek
and my voice is a house all on fire.

But for geography,
but for biology,
but for the way things happen,
it could have been

Unnamed female baby of the Abdul-Monim family.
Shot dead, Balal Ruz 22.1.2009.

you falling,
you holding your hand up for kissing.

Conversations with X and Y

I *Introductory interview*

When I heard they were coming, I ran.
You take your chances.
Sometimes you are seen. Sometimes not –

then you are not taken to a station
for the sin of your lipstick and whipped,
or slashed for an inch of flesh,

or blindfolded, dropped in a van,
kept in a single cell
and punched from behind, again, again;

your eyes are not injured,
your fingers broken; your private parts
hurt by a bottle.

You are allowed to use the toilet.
You are allowed to sleep.

*

Everything we did was underground.
Still, it was banned.
We earned nothing.

We were called
when they caught our friend.
No one under torture can keep silent.

So I left, like that –
a small bag
strapped to my back.

*

As you can imagine, I fled my country,
my family, for no good reason.
Many did not get out.

Some made it to Canada, which is safer.
We never intended Europe.
Europe is all closed doors.

Because our passports were false,
we were handcuffed.
Handcuffed and kept in a cell.

Five months.

*

I spent my whole life running
for speaking the truth.
Now it would seem

I never told the truth in all my life.
What I write does not exist
and when it does, I have not written it.

And so I am being sent back.
Having never written a word,
it is safe.

In our country, we had a choice
between the very bad
and the extremely.

For years,
I could not tell my own story.

When I did,
I could hardly breathe.

II *O Star*

based on the original by X

Say nothing, star – or they'll take you down.
We know the regime is rotten, but if you say it,
they'll have you. In an instant.
You know what that means, and it isn't good.
So keep shining, star, but do not speak.

Keep your thoughts to yourself,
little star. Don't shine too bright.
They have you in their sights
and you know what it is to be marked.
All that sky – and nowhere to hide.

Not for you. Death waits for us all,
it's true, but if you speak out,
it will come. All the quicker. So hush.
Concern yourself only with light,
with your twinkling.

There are men in their thousands,
now looking.
The mist hangs low in the garden.
The stars are all hidden.
They call for you

and you answer. Then a door slams shut
and the walls are white
and you cannot lie down
and there's a roof
where the sky should be, and a light

that will never (however you scream)
go out.

III *This is not a poem.*

Unfortunately, the story of your country is completely untranslatable.
Your language will never compute.
Your writing sets sail
to the wrong edge of the page
and no one will take it seriously.

When you speak, we cannot understand.
...the holy tree? the divine policy
of slicing a woman
for the sin of an inch of flesh?
Even in English, it makes no sense.

When you run through the streets
with your dead, their grey heads hanging,
the sound is gibberish.
All that heat.
You people should get a grip.

I have it on good authority
this is not how you say your own name.
As for poetry
I'd be shocked if you knew
how to write. Sign here. Here

in this country, we know how to treat
those who tell lies:
the pool on the pavement
which could not be blood,
or that thing in it, white (what *was* it?)–

those stories
I hear over and over, and still
I will not be moved.
I will not believe
that crap about singing, or that girl

(the one with the eyes), or this poem
(so-called) which is *nothing*,

nothing but words.

IV *Buried Alive*

based on the original by X

All this talk of crows
and still no harvest.

There's a slick on the land and it looks like oil
and no one can breathe the air
and still, the wind keeps on blowing
and whatever my country grows

is scattered. As I am,
at this time that should have been harvest.
I am thirty.
Do you need me to spell that out?

They ploughed my country by force
and I am a proud land
and will not spell out
what that means.

Trees do not die easily, as you know.
You have to work at it.
The axe is the easiest part.
Much harder to pull up the roots

but you did it,
you do it, you let it happen
with your eyes wide open,
you let it happen.

This is our Iran – and you smashed it.
This is our story – wound and salt.
Open wound.
Salt. Plenty of it.

Jude got an HGV licence

and drove abroad
with a lorry-load of food and clothes
through moonlit nights
of long, straight roads
and lines of lights.
Towns passed like pages, turned.

From some anonymously grim
Scouse home, Jude drove food
to the one old woman
left living on the mountain,
past blood sprayed black
up walls in empty houses;

stood accused in a Serbian court
of smuggling out a child,
and didn't feel afraid, but
guilty
because the boy never did
get away;

pissed in a margarine tub
when she couldn't leave the cab
for fear of mines; took clothes
to the rape-camp survivors.
The eyes
she would never forget.

And back in Blighty,
was tranquillised
and hospitalised
and electrocuted discreetly
in the head
for her own good.

On waking,
she was a tree-trunk split by lightning;
a quarry after the dynamite.
she was a house with the fire put out.
She couldn't hold a cigarette
for shaking.

Now tell me.

Where are you in this story?
Did you stand in front of the guns?
Were you helpless?
Has it ever been your blood
up the wall?
Were you the judge

or the camp guard sipping his tea?
When the switches were flicked,
when the walls were constructed,
and the rifles were loaded and cocked and then pointed –
when the court stood to order,
when the nurse came to take her

with a tick list of names
and the last one said *Jude*
and the windows were locked
and the ward clock was pointing at quarter past two –
where in this poem –
in the world –

where were you?

Going going

Now there's a space, a dappled green space
where a tree used to fit,
where the leaves hushed and shifted
and the sound was all liquid
where I lay in the shade
before words.

Now a sweet space
where the loganberries ripened,
and a high wall was standing around our garden
and the neighbour threw coals
that frightened our chickens
and my father shook trees for the pears

and my mother broke ice for the birds in the winter
and scooped dough from the loaves
and cut rind from the bacon.
And for all of my children –
a space for them too, and their voices
and faces.

A space for a budgie, a tortoise called
Tolly. A space for a war
and whatever came after.
For towers and planes crashing over and over.
For how the reservoir looked in the winter.
For Soviet Russia, the spires and soldiers,

the Russian for music,
instructions to play it. An alphabet. Two.
For bank book and debit,
the concept of credit, for cash and
where is it.
For the cot in my bedroom

and who was it filled it?
For the sell-by-date
and today's date
and have-I-eaten-yet.
For whatever I did
in the last five minutes.

Several dozen spaces
for my friends.

Cupboard

Of course I know where I am
exactly, on what floor
and who is running the country.
It is my country,

my parents bowling a kiss
down a lane for a blonde girl to catch.
Where is she?
Can I count backwards from twenty?

There's a hole where something was
and it keeps me awake.
Mornings, I think in dreams,
a cold street, me in my nightie

and a man who was never my father
shouting over and over
I don't know where the handle is,
or the light.

There was something
I came downstairs for,
Can you tell me?
Someone put the wrong stuff

in all of my drawers
or in that thing, whatever it is
(remind me)
that *thing* you keep cups in.

French lesson

You used to be able to talk this language
if not fluently, then
enough to get by.

You conversed on more than the weather,
the time, the size of your town.
How many rooms has your house?

Now
it is slipping away.
Until someone asks the wrong question,

you don't realise what you've lost.
Not just the objects – keys,
baby, car – but what is the word

for air?
You ought, you ought
to know this. It will not come.

It has gone.
Some of it so recently,
you can still feel its shape in your mouth.

So much you still want to say.
But the wrong language
simply will not do.

So you find yourself
in a crowded shop
scrabbling for the right words

like coins
and like coins
you just don't have them.

Everyone
is watching it happen.

Ewe

Now she is on her knees
with the foot-rot; the hot infection
streaking silver to the hip.
With the throb and the weight
of her hedge-heavy fleece –
all moss, twig and grease, old rain.

She is losing it, losing it. The
lamb-leap and skip – all her fastness,
back from the day when touch came
pink, milk dripping,
back in the days of gangs, when
she was Spring

and nothing more; allbody,
air green wind blue grass –
how the wind took her up by the heels,
heartflip, tripped her,
from one wall off to its opposite.
Loving it. Loving it.

Unhappy animal – she does not want
what this is: the deep autumn dip
and the flounder, this winter:
how grass now is food, regardless;
hedge is fence; and wall –
wall is where it all stops.

Shorn. Unrecognisable.
How, with mere days passing,
did this happen?
This is not her skin – or yours either.
She wants it back:
her coat, her old turf, self –

what brought her flock to this,
down from the hills, to dwindle?
This winter could see them all dead –
one more blunder
under the lip of a crag, rockfast,
neck-deep in a bog.

Losing it.
Losing the plot.
Tell me, when did you lose it
– the power of thought?
Where did you put it?
Where did you last have it?

Night

Is sleeping house. Is stars and trees.
Is distant noise of trains and cars.
Is ice and broken skies. Is bruise.

Is still backstreets in silent Burnley,
lights shimmering across the valley.
Is memory. Is always lonely.

Is motorway and shoulder-ache,
is travel sick and ciggie smoke,
is no idea where to go,

is keep on driving
night

is heading south, is heading north,
is mouth on mouth, is steady breath,
is teeth is knife is

a brown clock in a heavy room.
A full moon gleaming like a scream.
Is itchy covers empty pages flowers dead in stinking vases

is corridors and plastic doors,
unwashed floors and no-sleep faces.
Lifts with electronic voices

Is strip lights and locked tight.
Always night.
Back-lit and never-black.

Deadly as a cigarette
without the recompense of light.
Is keep on driving.

Night.

Tree

Tonight, Tree is very tired
of being Tree.
Tree wants to be something else.

Not another kind of tree, but
something different entirely –
like a dachshund

on a quiet summer's morning in Tokyo
with an owner who knows nothing
of wood.

Tonight, Tree aches,
the way a cello does, or blood.
She cannot be comforted.

Tree wants no one to touch her or hold her
though she yearns for it more than the world.
Sick of the company of trees,

she loathes their steadfast insistence
on distance and closeness.
Their earnest intent to do good.

Tree is finished with goodness,
with Spring's showy brightness.
She does not feel at home

except in Winter.
She is jealous of birds
and the air.

Tree will fly sometime
if it kills her. But not tonight.
She is done with trying so hard.

Tree wants to lie.
Tree wants to be irresponsible and inconsequential.
Tree wants to do wicked things.

She doesn't know what they are yet
but she sees them inside her
like rooks.

Tonight,
in the deep of the forest,
Tree itches and whispers

like a ship for a storm,
for something to sink her
or save her or change her.

Or failing that,
sleep.

Or failing that,
light.

STREET POETRY

No 3: KEN

Soup

How much love
in a neat white shirt, a
tin of soup, reheated?

It was like holding meat,
how she'd lie there and would not answer.
I began to forget how to speak.

No more the stars. No more the low hills
where we watched the city glisten,
no more the electric air,

the pub lights swimming with colour,
the ceiling
spinning us off towards bed,

together. Her shoulder.
The intricate spread
of her toes.

How she was a book I read over and over
and how she called out
like pain.

I am tired of being alone.
I want stars in their perfect formations.
I want that woman.

Not this.
In me, there is a whole street
empty.

A city I walk through,
mostly at night.
Mostly, it rains.

No 5: JOHN

Hands up

– who hasn't wanted
to graze with a finger
untouchable treasure –

some creamy-white sculpture?
When told off – to back off –
to get your damn hands off –

whose mouth has not watered?
And who has not craved
whatever's forbidden –

the fruit in the garden –
to stuff it all in
when nobody's looking?

Who's never considered
another man's dinner –
to taste for yourself,

to sink in the teeth,
to dig in the knife?
Who's not in love with

Keep Out – Do Not Enter?
Who's never been drawn
to swim in deep water?

Deep down in your centre
who's not a believer,
a schemer, a scammer,

a Heathcliff, a dreamer?
Who's never – however one-off –
been a sinner?

Who never messed up
in spectacular manner?
Who's ever confessed with no need?

Hands up, that man
who would truly refuse it – over and over –
if offered it all on a plate.

If you were to ask it –
was it all worth it,
to have it, to lose it

the wage in my pocket,
the girlfriend, the lover –
I'd tell you a secret

(come closer, come closer):
I'd do it – again
and again – in a minute...

No 7: LIAM

I heard it

before it reached me. Even before
his car started up –
(I was ordering the first round) –

I heard him wake up
to the black static shock of a radio clock;
the crack of his wrists as he lifted;
the high complaint of his cat.

His kettle? A plane taking off
at least three times over.
The rumble of water, his deepening bath.
His gobbing, his coughing, his piss.
On my third pint by now (stag night, remember?)
I heard the latch, lifted.
Three locks.

The separate fall
of their separate pieces.
The echo of steps in the hall;
the whispery drift of litter in corners.
I was leaving the pub. The ceiling was moving,
the stars slightly swaying.
Heard the car. Starting.

His foot on the pedals,
the air in his nostrils,
his hands deadly quiet on the wheel.
I was out on the street
and the sky was a map
and the streetlights were polished like stars.
A scream as he sped

round the corner.
In the glare of my head
it was suddenly summer;
my mother was sleeping,
(son husband lover)
(son husband lover)
you could hear the stream laughing
where we used to fish.

(Somebody calling.)

My name being spoken
again and again.
(A door, very quietly, closing
and locking).
Night – and rain –
falling.
Night and rain falling.

No 8: JOE

But drowning

Forgot how to smile, forgot how to eat,
how to talk straight, how to walk down the street
without my own breath
balled hard in my gut;
my heart, a tight knot in my throat.

Forgot how my eyes
had not always hurt; how the light
was not always too bright
or colours too sharp
or a hand on my arm much too hard.

Forgot that my hands could be warm,
that my blood could run hot, forgot
how to lie in the night
with a woman to warm me and nothing to harm me.
and nothing to make it all stop (or rewind) –

and nothing to make it all stop.
Forgot there's a limit – what one man can take –
the pain in my neck, in my back; I forgot
there was ever a time
that my hands didn't shake.

Forgot how to sleep
without running, to dream without falling,
to wake without gasping
like breaking the skin of a lake every morning.
The unbreakable skin of a lake.

The weeds in the dark
slowly turning and rotting, the cold shadows shifting,
the cold horrors growing.
Nameless things brushing my legs.
And always there, waiting –

a current to seize me and freeze me and take me
out way too far. Way too deep.

No 13: CLAIRE

Cuckoo

At two a.m,
night meant little more
than strip lights and no cars.

Ten eyes staring, urgently,
me at their centre
when he burst raggedly from me, wet

and I was a fire extinguished,
and never alone
in this world again.

The small heat of his body
on my skin.

Now

I pull on my smile each day
like someone else's clothes.
I am okay, I say. But nothing fits.

I am okay, I say
through each meal cooked,
each nappy taped. It's easy, easy,

easy. But in the park
the trees do not make any sense
and the hedges are all grey.

You see, the exact shape of gulls
flying threewards in an ill sky,
the language of signs in the café

all confirm what I know already.
This baby is strangely heavy.
His fingers are unwelcome.

His smile is forged. He is lying
all wrong in my arms.
His smell – wool, milk –

is baby,
but not mine.
Not mine at all.

A roof. And the whole of the city
spelled in light
and the wind slapping at my face

over and over
and nobody calling my name
but my baby, who is never asleep

in my arms.
And everyone in on it.
And nowhere to go.

U

is not flat. Is not bright
like an apple, a laugh. Is sure
and predictable, sturdy. A trough
with the bucket still in it.
All things in their place
and the right way to say it.

Is muddy and mucky and tough.
Not little and timid, polite –
U is scooped out, the shape of a mug;
a hook or a loop in a gut;
a rut in a churned-up track.
Earthy and turfy, well-dug.

Not scared of dirt, U is
stubble and grunt, a good fuck,
drunk. A mouth full of tongue
or a curse. For better or worse
and as trusted as blood.
Not flat –

U is a stomach stuffed tight
as a drum. Warm houses
all in a huddle by night.
Undeniably home.
If rough's what you mean,
then say it.

Likewise plum.

Recording crime

When the words are taken away
what you're left with
is a young man's body over yours;
his hands on your mouth
like bricks; the bricks

of his lips on your mouth.
What you're left with is
the sun, not caring
what he does or doesn't do
to you; specifically, whether

you die.
When the words are all gone,
what's left
is a brief run-through of your life
unfolding behind your eyes;

and how afterwards, not stopping
to brush the dust from your legs,
you tried to think logically
of the next step
which – logically – was seeking help.

When the words are taken away
you're left with a room
and a woman who smelt like your mother.
How the words
you thought you should say

weren't what you wanted
at all. Not like
early that day in the lake
when water meant cold stuff
that dazzled your body.

Grass smelt yellow,
blanket was home.
Trees were a shade
that you walked through
and Clare was your name

and meant you.

This isn't

what mothers are meant to do.
They're not meant to stand in the corner
of a white room
while their daughters are led, bewildered
to a white couch covered in paper;

to not say a word
as their daughters are stripped
over floor-sized sheets of paper
and the paper gathered and saved;
the daughters laid out, naked;

their injuries duly noted
(marks to the neck; abrasions);
they're not meant to see
those horrible swabs on sticks
or the places they were poked.

This isn't what mothers should do.
They should be home, cooking broth;
washing kids in steamy baths;
de-thorning roses; waiting for daughters
who don't come back

from five-minute bike rides to churchyards
where boys with shaven heads are waiting
to pick them up
like flightless birds
who can't do anything but flap.

They should be at home
with bags full of knitting;
a kiss. The mothers know it.
They want to be anywhere,
anywhere but this.

The no baby poem

There will be no ceremony
in a quiet wood for this. Today,
the sun does not matter.
You have simply not made it
into existence. All science, all alchemy
have failed from the start.
There is only this
injury, nameless and wet.

You are everything I know now
of loss, the perfect
grey weight of it, constant,
which has turned down the light
in my face.

Had just one moment
of one month been different,
you would have been born
into winter.
We would have made the drive
in the late afternoon,
past front rooms in Luddenden
yellow with warmth
a jewellery of light in each window
to see you erupt like summer
into our hands.

No-show, non-event,
we have lost you
to a world where there is no word,
even for absence.
Whatever could have made you
is irrelevant. Today,
the slightest breeze could blow me
clean away.

You

are the size of a large strawberry
and around you, I am
world. Quite literally.
My belly is bedrock
and all the night sky.

And though you don't know
the feel of the breeze yet,
I am rain, and all of your weathers.
What light you have
is through my skin.

Now you have ears,
I am a country in progress around them.
In me, strata are formed and exploded.
I am river
and the way all waters move.

Soon, you will be the size of a lemon.
And above you, I will be landscape
where factories hum and small towns fume
and votes are cast
for the wrong kind of people.

Small fruit, you
are my mineral wealth
and you will not be exploited.
My heart is an industry
that never shuts down.

My bad knees are Atlas
supporting the planet, and my hands
are huge ships
that will carry you, sleeping,
into the night, out

into the starlit world.

Not baby, nor boy

(for Billy)

nor even animal. You are more tadpole,
a comical miracle. A thin white shoot
at the root of a small Spring plant.
Amazingly breakable, brave.

Little more than a shape
made of light.
Ancient outsider – stranger
to our worn, familiar planet –

this is not to say
that you put it all into perspective.
The world is entirely unswerved
by your arrival:

worms are elastically tugged from their tunnels,
rain glides sideways
on the same roads over the moors,
planes scorch through the same blue skies.

The airwaves still crowded
with death and bad news;
the old drinking songs from the nineties –
Michael continues to lose his religion

but now it's me in the corner,
the planet of your skull in my hand
as you dangle your left leg over my finger
which under your knee

is tree-trunk and oak, is heavyweight lifter,
is beam, joist and girder,
is God's good pink finger
bringing the world into being,

is holding you sleeping, is keeping
the whole sky from falling.

You took a tumble

(for Billy)

and almost fell out of the world.
Do you remember –
how night suddenly gripped you
and would not let go its hold?

Was it deep waters where no sunlight reaches;
a corridor – you at the end?
A fast road dizzy with lights
speeding you off

to some place where no one could follow?
What creatures did you meet there,
what far, exotic stars
when you fell to the floor

and kept falling?

One small trip took you
so almost-completely
it should have been cliff-top, fiftieth storey,
or a well-shaft, deep as an eye.

You fell

where no one could reach you
no coal-dusted rescuers
could blast through that rock.
No rope could haul you back up.

Your mothers could send you no oranges.
No man could be lowered on winches to lift you
or covered in butter
and pushed through a small gap to save you.

Floodlights flicked on
as that grim dusk descended
which did not lift for months
until you came up –

paler and thinner, bewildered
by the stars where they waited
and shivered in hundreds,
by the roar of the floodlit crowd.

Vow

Say yes.
That word on your lips
is a kiss;
is a promise already made.
We made it.

Love did not turn from hurt
or hard work.
When lights failed, it did not switch off.
When love had no road,
we willingly built it.

We shouldered its stones
and its dirt. So thank god
there are days like this when it's easy.
When we open our mouths
and the words flood in.

Put the word of your hand
in mine.

We have learnt to hold to each other
when nothing was given by right;
how love will insist
with its ache; with its first painful
tug on the guts;

its snake in the nest of the ribs;
the bomb in the chest;
in the Y of the thighs; the red, red
red sun of it, rising.
How love must, at all costs,

be answered. We have answered
and so have a million before us
and each of their names is a vow.

So now I can tell you, quite simply
you are the house I will live in:

there is no good reason
to move. Good earth,
you are home, stone, sun,
all my countries. Vital to me
as the light. You are it

and I am asking.
Say yes.

Love opens a door
then slams it. It does.
It loses its touch and its looks.
But love needs its fury.
We have fought

and when times make it necessary,
we will again. When night draws in,
we won't forget
how once the streets ran wet with light
and love. Like blood. They will again.

But for now,
we make our promises gently.
This extraordinary day we have made.
Listen –
the birds in their ordinary heaven.

Tonight the sky will blaze
with stars. Today, my love,
rooms bloom with flowers.
Say yes.
The sky is ours.

The Lesbian Guide to Conception.

The moon has not bothered
to set today
but is one small cloud
in a sky like a mile of sea.

She has not seen her first summer
or autumn yet, or the silver-soft days
of earliest winter. She might expect
world always grows hotter,

nights ever lighter;
that nothing is ever complete.
She closes her eyes in Liverpool,
wakes in Italy –

all is equally strange.
At ten thousand feet
she's transfixed by her fingers
the astonishing crackle

of plastic and paper.
Clouds stacked higher
than rubble or sugar
lie unnoticed outside the plane.

*

So many surfaces
and all of them alive.
Air is wetter than breath
and warm as a bath;

the bright lake is heavy with cold.
Huge birds glide
at knee height.
Fish are the colour of flame

and under her feet –
the perfect, mouth-shaped
shape of a stone.
A single boat nods to the waves.

Italy stops in the street
to greet her – 'Ciao, Bella!'
She answers, fluent
in the language of water,

the chatter of jasmine and birds.
Italy melts in her mouth, cold-sweet,
wakes her each night
with its heat, sheets wet,

her small back spangled with sweat.
Arms wide,
she blesses the night
as she sleeps.

*

How did you go about it?

We climbed alone
to the top
of a very steep hill.
No path.

Not a map or a compass
between us.
We left no word
of our route.

Light greyed,
then faded. Mist fell thick,
and with it, night.
Dark seemed to go on

forever.
Sometimes, we heard voices, caught

occasional glimpses of colour.
We did not recognise a thing.

After several years, it lifted.
Then the landscape breathed in
oh – like this –
and it wasn't our hill anymore,

no, this was a different valley
entirely.
No,
this was a different country.

*

How did you – actually – go about it?

Sunday evening. Caught a train
to London. Slept alone.
Woke to the sound
of next door's alarm.

The usual darkness.
Hotel room.
Opened the curtain.
Light poured in.

*

How was the birth?

She came to us in December
over a lake of angry water
like a storm
or the first day breaking.

I was broken in two completely
and she –
she was what they discovered
inside me.

Ewe in several parts

I lost my baby.
I left her outside for a moment,
in her seat, out, over the fence.
I could see her –
she was playing with her feet, she was singing.

There were lambs in the field
and two sheep.
I went upstairs for a moment.
When I came back
she was gone.

There were sheep in the field.
One took her.
Up to the woods where the ferns uncoil,
where the water spills in ledges
down the hill

and no one has seen her since,
no sign.
Only the mud and the empty grey seat;
the wool in the hedge,
a message.

*

Who else would have taken my baby?
Do you want me to tell you
it was ants, it was worms,
it was birds swooped down,
the metal-blue birds that live under the bridge –

that they came in a pair and lifted her
one underneath each arm,
flew her back to their nest lined with feathers;
they feed her tiny white fish
that catch in her throat like coins?

But my daughter is a big girl,
a solid girl, she cannot fly.

I should know. I carried her,
ten months riding inside me,
my belly stretched and itching, each morning
hoisting her from sleep, my back
like an old bridge aching. I should know.

I cannot sneeze without remembering
the dark nest of her head in my pelvis,
how for months I could not stand.

*

My baby has gone.
I left her outside for a minute,
I could hear if she cried. She did not.

She must have liked it,
her hands tangled deep in the sheep's deep wool
where the moss and the small twigs snag.

She must have liked it
the way she likes dogs,
her hands to its mouth and stamping

just like she does when she's pleased:
a lift packed with light arrives at her face,
the doors separate, the light spills out.

My daughter is feeding on the wrong kind of milk:
chalky, lemony-sour.
It will make her sick.

*

Was it my fault?
I took her up to the woods in my arms,
I sat with her, held branches down to her.

I fed her there by the water.
I showed her the buds and the ferns.

She pushed her hands into the mulch,
she knew the touch of stone. I laid her in grass
from the day she was born.
She loved the light, the trees spidering out,
the sound of the birds and the breezes.

I thought I was doing right.
Maybe I wanted her gone.
There was a day when the rains came steaming
and we walked by the river
and her face was wet and my face was wet

and I thought of throwing her in,
there where the black water rages.
I wanted to poke my mind out
and make it gone forever.
I thought of throwing her in the river.

*

People look at my face and see lies.
When she was taken
I didn't look the right way, I didn't cry.
Some don't.
When I heard that my father was dead,

I laughed, I thought of Christmas.
I did not cry for days
and then only when his photograph
went bobbing down the river,
when it wouldn't sink.

And yes, it is true, I said it:
she is not my baby. I meant this:
she grew inside me, I fed her,
I do not own her. I saw this from birth
when they laid her on me

and she was hard and damp
and would not stay still.
She has her own blood,
her eyes like fish,
her own bright cheek, her mouth.

They say I have hidden her
in a mattress, she lives in there
for hours at a time. She plays with the springs,
it smells of piss and feathers.
I will not let her out.

*

Some people say she was taken.

I have thought of a woman
in a lodge made of wood
where the sun shines all night in the winter
and the sea moves in lines
of silver and black
and she is raising my baby.

I do not believe this is true.

Some say she was taken
by people who mean her great harm.
When I think of this
there is nothing to see but dust.
I think in sounds that don't
make sense, I cannot breathe.

Some people say she is dead.

But my daughter is okay,
I know it. I would feel it
if there was anything different
but all I feel now is the gap. I carry it with me.
People do not know where to look.
They smell the loss on me

like mist.

Each day I count my blessings.
My daughter is okay.

*

She is near me –
up in the woods with the sheep.
It lays her on moss, on the grass,
it wipes the milk from her face
with its fleece. It (very carefully)
chews her nails.

My daughter is okay. She is not far from me.
She watches the sky break with rain.
The sheep comforts her, and my girl
is not afraid. She twists her fingers
into its wool, she pulls its ears.
She smiles and the sheep smiles too.

My daughter is okay, I am proof.
If she were not okay I would not be alive.
But I am.

I welcome the warm days
when she plays with the lambs:
now she can crawl, they teach her to kick.
I welcome the soft days of leaves,
she can fall and the ground will not hurt her.
In winter, I pray for her

like mad.

*

I know she will come back.

I saw what the police did
with their signs, their concerned faces,

their lowered voices. I saw what they did
with their tweezers, their little pots.
I heard what they said.

But I am her mother
and I know better.

I know because of this.
I ran into the field that morning,
wearing only my feet.
The grass was bright and wet.
Carefully I gathered the fleece,

the mud and the water, the small stream
running in ledges,
carefully I gathered each ant.
I laid them together.
At first they made no sense

but then you could see it, clear as anything
and the breeze was blowing, it smelt of her
and the birds were calling
and whichever way I looked at them,
they spelt it out, clear and clean

as light.
Then I knew for sure
where my baby had gone.

I am her mother.
It is my job to believe.

In the space of that year

14th January: I register her birth, which is to say
somebody writes it on paper.
My face is a cave.
We walk round town but nowhere's open.

She hangs from me; small weight. I'm meat,
heavier than you'd think was possible.
Each night, she drifts in her basket
through waves of colourless sleep

I can hardly believe anymore.
She's a small cat curled at my chest,
searching for breast like air,
her mouth, its entire own creature.

Nobody told us a thing:
that mouth and its hunger
and nothing to fill it
but me –

that mouth like a punishment – nobody warned us;
counting her life up
in gulps – fifty-nine, sixty –
in the open-and-shut (third time this night)

of her breakable throat.

*

So world emerged
from the winter we willed her into,
its lights, its forests of noises
(she could not focus, she did not know us);

colour belled and pressed
like hands heeled hard against her eyes,

glowing like pain or clouds of stars,
like blood or Spring arriving.

World took shape
in air and its textures
she was pushed through or lifted;
she slavered and slept, she was still

and the silence was bees.
Her arms were Africa.
Her legs were Russia. Her back was
Here Be Monsters

and though there had always been voices,
it was out of the dream
world reached her
with the cold plastic skin of a mat.

With light.
With hunger and faces;
the absence of water;
with dog, and the shock of a sneeze.

She could not sit up or eat.
Could not speak.
She could not lift her own head.
She could not find her feet

until she did

She's waited half her life to write this.

She's stalled for years, claiming
the weather was not right,
the sky the wrong shade,
the morning/day/night
much too short. The week was always
too full, or the year.

Then it came to her,
one afternoon, when the child
was in nursery, the cat
rattling its dish beside her, the floor
clean enough for now
that she could no longer avoid it.

This is your pen, she said, and
you can make anything happen

or unhappen.

A withered brown flower takes on new colour

the way sky does at dawn, or paper drinks water.
So the burial party walks back to the church
with its shocking, heart-stopping mahogany coffin

where the organ is playing 'Abide with Me' backwards;
unneeded umbrellas are solemnly folded;
the pall-bearers shoulders relieved of their burden,

and funeral coats of their rain.
All through the service no one will notice
that nothing the priest says make any sense.

Back at the house all the lights are still on;
the quiches and hams and the cakes are uneaten;
the bottles of sherry and port are unopened, the glasses not broken,

no beer-sodden uncles are waltzing with nieces,
no carpets are stained by spilt wine.
All fond and inaccurate memories unspoken,

all secretive aunts can hang on to their secrets,
uncomfortable histories will not be rewritten
in freshly-mopped kitchens.

By the mid-morning, the priest is retreating
back to the vestuary, quickly disrobing
then waking up late

from strong drink and bad dreaming
refusing his supper, a half-hour unwriting
the funeral sermon.

So you're riding the hearse to her house in reverse,
wiping the dust back on to the surfaces
unbaking cakes, scraping butter from sandwiches,

reshelving the port and the good cut-glass glasses,
making up beds with used sheets.
Replacing her papers, her dresses on hangers.

Taking her shoes back out of their boxes.

Ocixem

*A pacifist, indigenous group, Las Abejas stood in solidarity with the
aims of the Zapatista uprising. On 1997, in Acteal, 45 members of
the group were shot dead by state-supported paramilitaries. 35 of the
dead were women; the youngest child to die was eight months old.*

Sixteen Dutch tourists are filling their glasses
and night flowers close as late evening approaches
and the streets of San Cristóbal fill.
Musicians walk back to unpack their instruments
for drunken encores in closing-time restaurants
and thirsty beer-drinkers exit the bars.
Stars circle the sky the wrong way

and all day, the buses empty and fill,
things are broken and spilt
and set right again in similar numbers,
fake amber bracelets sold back to the vendors,
to underage girls who look like their mothers
with overage faces in oversize dresses.

Soon, afternoon diners are filling their dishes
with postres and dulces and courses of carnes,
and baskets are filled with warming tortillas
and uneaten dishes of sopa de lima
are carried away by underpaid waiters
as meals are uncooked by the chef.

By noon, streets are packed
with hornblowing traffic
inch-by-inch backwards unmaking their journeys
and thousands of coffees
returned to the cafés

and across the Chiapas, masked Zapatistas
ask federal armies to stay a while longer
as communal corn is restored by the soldiers
and indigenous people return to their villages,

to their undestroyed houses
from ankle-deep camps
where no child ever died of a curable illness

and outside Oaxaca
the desaparecidos walk home to their families
and the streets and the lorries are emptied of bodies
and government promises are made and unbroken
and you can imagine

how women and children
are helped to their feet by the butt of a gun
how women and children face-down in the mud
in the temperate rain and the muck and the blood
could rise to their knees with their clothes all unstained

and soldiers are taking their fingers off triggers;
young soldiers replacing the guns in their holsters
and forty-five heads left intact
which, several hours later
are fondled and braided by unknowing mothers,
the dead sitting down to their usual breakfast.

Irreversible

there is no wound that won't heal
I told myself that day
and still repeat it from time to time
but not enough to believe it.

CHARLOTTE DELBO 1995

I

If we believe the screen,
she is thin
and younger than thirty.

In reality, she's overweight.
Her hair
has always been short.

In the film, which most of us
will not bring ourselves to watch,
her hand is outstretched.

In reality, she's ten.
In her fist,
there's a bunch of leaves.

In the film,
there's a sound like slapping: wet,
somewhat incidental.

In reality, it is like this
except all she can think of
is how much it hurts.

In the film, she is in a subway.
The viewer imagines the smell:
concrete and dirt; sour fruit.

In reality, there is sun.
She is a five-minute bike ride
from home

under the town's tallest steeple.
In the film
(as you'll now remember)

she is crying
before anything even begins.
She will not call him Daddy.

In reality,
she'll do anything. Anything
to survive.

II

For the putting together of cars after crashes,
we have tow trucks and menders and beaters and welders,
scrappies and vendors, second-hand dealers,
various healers for any survivors – ambulance drivers,
women in dresses with needles and stitches,
the men in white coats and the cleaners of messes.

For the fixing of harm, we have doctor and surgeon,
the right operation, the miracle potion.
Prayers to Saint Jude and divine intervention.
State institutions – the locked ward and prison,
Criminal Injuries Board Compensation
(12 grand for a hand or a limb amputation).

For any dilemma, the relevant answer –
the plaster, the hammer, the handcuff, the razor.
Gear for all weathers, fire for cold winters,
high-factor sun-cream for holiday-makers;
carbon offsetters for drivers and jetters.
On every street we've a light for the darkness.

To make it all better, the talkers and listeners;
the bakers of cakes and committed fundraisers,
savers of schools and community centres;
rebuilders of homes and the lifters of faces;
starters of hearts and replacers of parts –
toupees and teeth and pacemakers.

For all types of anguish, the product to end it;
all nature of damage, the person to mend it.
Hope for the hopeless and
speech for the speechless.
For every harm, its reverse.
And then this.

III

No one can stop them.
They were always going
to wake; but still, let the sun
take its usual path in reverse;
let small birds baffle the sky.

At what point should we hit rewind?
At the start of the night
– with the enviable feat
of returning a cork to its bottle?
Or at the morning's first light?

Do we strip them completely-
unzip that skirt
which was clearly too small?
Leave the T-shirt and shorts on the floor?
Hit pause

as the latch is lifted – keep them there,
caught on their doorsteps forever,
feet flexed at the heel for stepping?
At least for that evening,
that bright summer's morning.

Believe me. We do have a duty to stop this.
But don't stop that woman from drinking.
We know exactly what's coming. So
pour her one more, more,
more. She cannot make fresh decisions.

She will always take that subway in the dark;
the film dictates, and in reality
that girl will ride to the church in her shorts
on her silver-blue, nearly-new bike.
Oh, make her turn back

to the light, where the people are,
the cars still unfeasibly passing.
A man has his hand on her neck.
There is always some button –
quick, hit it.

We do not need to see this –
whichever direction this is played
there is only a blip in the terrible rhythm
those terrible sounds,
like choking, like slapping –

there will never be sense
in the words she is screaming.

IV

It's easy enough –
the cleaning of messes;
high-pressure hoses take blood out of stone.

Even the smell
can be dealt quite simply. And really
there never was that much to see –

a shape in the dirt
gone one strong rain later.
A wall, which was always unchanged.

Not much to undo then. Only the flats –
the breezeblocks and scaffold,
the rafters and struts.

Only the bushes to cut;
the birds (which had never stopped singing)
to fill in the gap;

the path that she took
to be ravelled right up;
the cars to return where they came from;

the dust to lay down on the track.
Only the church to pull up by its roots;
only the roof to rip back;

only the police to retreat to the station;
the night sky
emptied of traffic and siren.

Only that girl to stand up.

V

From where they're both lying –
flat with the dry twigs sharp in her back
or face to the brutal stone –

it's a matter of order.
As the subway grows soft
and returns to the mixer;

and the sky now can enter –
and there's nobody there
but her and the stars

wheeling and racing and dying above her,
not understanding a thing
so we'll let her

return to that morning,
the bedroom she shared
with her next-but-one sister.

Let her wake on a morning too warm for pyjamas;
four books stuffed under
her understuffed pillow;

let her lie for a while:
the beginnings of summer,
the holidays spread like a blanket beneath her,

the days without edges;
under the soft roofs
of churches and bushes

where birds are conversing
and beetles are shifting the earth
with their jaws;

where days drift in voices
from gardens and parks that go on for ever
to houses made golden with dust.

Let her have it:
falling in slabs from the window above her;
dripping from leaves in the silence of morning;

spilling in torrents on eye, fur and feather;
spreading, a bruise,
like blood dropped in water.

Light.
Enough to believe it.
And never forget it.

You'd start with the page

which would spread the full length and the height of the wall
and the hall, out, into the Halifax street,
over the cars and the two blocks of flats,
the pubs and cheap shops and out of the town –
Ovenden, Mixenden, Luddenden Foot –
over the tips and the burnt-out wrecks,
coating the lakes like leathery ice

where the ducks and geese would circle, bewildered
as the great sheet of paper breathed over the water –
rolling on beyond Yorkshire and over the borders
to Lancashire, Lincolnshire, Durham and Cumbria.
The newbuild estates in the floodplains of Cheshire
would wake to a drift banked up at the doors
and the windows half-blinded and white.

Soon, roads would be blocked from here to the Highlands –
from Skerry to Scourie and Smoo to Achfary –
paper falling in swathes over Wales, on to Ireland,
stilling the oil rigs, grounding the ferries,
confounding the lighthouse man beyond Lundy
as the whitest of silence swept down
on the seas.

No moment's pause for convenience or safety –
all major cities suddenly stalled,
both Houses recalled, the army deployed
on behalf of the nation by brave politicians;
government holed in a bunker somewhere.
All our great thinkers with no explanation
for the huge white page and no words

as the paper rolled on, on, out –
over the heat of the Gobi, Death Valley,
the colour and gunshots in Mexico City:
obscuring the birth of a million new babies,
over shanty-town poverty, officeblock money,

and more – the sour brown roar
of the Amazon, Nile,

mile after mile after mile
after mile.

Astronauts
afloat in their stations
would watch, white-faced, as the marble-blue earth
paled to a perfect pearl, to a tooth,
to a clean light, cold as a knife.
At this height

you could trace with a finger
the borders of nations, the muscle and surge
of covered-up oceans; the protrusion of peaks
from blanketed mountains.
The silence is almost
complete.

No one can hear it –
six billion voices (including your mother's);
the names being called in four thousand languages.
Not the scratching of nails on ungiving walls,
nor the catch of your own front door.
At this height,

you could blank it all out
– with one hand – like the light.
There's no one would blame you.
There's many might thank you.
At this distance,
you could live with it

for a minute.
Then you'd pick up your pen.
And write.

www.ingramcontent.com/pod-product-compliance
Lightning Source LLC
Jackson TN
JSHW080855211224
75817JS00002B/53